UN-ORTHODOX
BOY

God bring colour to your soul

Michael Jones

UN-ORTHODOX BOY

Michael James

iUniverse, Inc.
Bloomington

Un-Orthodox Boy

Copyright © 2011 by Michael James.

All rights reserved. No part of this book may be used or reproduced by any means, graphic, electronic, or mechanical, including photocopying, recording, taping or by any information storage retrieval system without the written permission of the publisher except in the case of brief quotations embodied in critical articles and reviews.

iUniverse books may be ordered through booksellers or by contacting:

iUniverse
1663 Liberty Drive
Bloomington, IN 47403
www.iuniverse.com
1-800-Authors (1-800-288-4677)

Because of the dynamic nature of the Internet, any web addresses or links contained in this book may have changed since publication and may no longer be valid. The views expressed in this work are solely those of the author and do not necessarily reflect the views of the publisher, and the publisher hereby disclaims any responsibility for them.

Any people depicted in stock imagery provided by Thinkstock are models, and such images are being used for illustrative purposes only. Certain stock imagery © Thinkstock.

ISBN: 978-1-4620-2971-6 (pbk)
ISBN: 978-1-4620-2973-0 (ebk)

Printed in the United States of America

iUniverse rev. date: 06/24/2011

CONTENTS

BIRD & WATER XI

And God Loves All His Ducks 1
Ha-Mayim min Ha-Shamyim 5
Halcyon 8
Meddling with Water 10
Ptarmigan 12
Deplore 13
Sitta canadensis 14
Offering 15
Dance of the Elements 16
Unwanted Splash 17

AMOUR & BEAUTY 19

Wine 21
Cavorting 22
Caramel Flavoured Dark Roast 23
Balance 25
Cloth 27
Wednesday at 1 o'clock 28
Song of the Magpie 29
Love So Great 31
Academics 32

FAITH & ACHE 35

Driving the Dirt Road 37
Spin Straw into Gold 39

Tarnish 41
A Bird Then Gone 44
Captivated 46
Arrow 47
Adam Song 49
Psalmofnosleep 50
Eucharist 51
Within the Attic 52

DREAM & ELUSION 53

Lines Written in Response to a Children's Book 55
Glámur - an Icelandic Song I Listened to 56
My Memory in History 57
Whatever–ness & Realisms 58
Non–Wine Drinker 60
Pens That Make Poems Better 62
Come, Green 63
The Question Still Stands 64
At the Opera 65
My Prayer 66

FRIEND & QUIRK 69

Childhood Fiddle-faddle 71
Un-Orthodox Boy 72
Publication 73
Follow Me 74
Inquietude 75
Perception 77
Within the Second Floor Vault 79
Deep Mistake 80
Would God Fly a Kite? 81
More Than a Poem 83

For brothers Wright
with love

Most people ignore most poetry
because
most poetry ignores most people.

~Adrian Mitchell (1932-2008)

Bird & Water

And God Loves All His Ducks

mallards outside the library
two of them
yes that is right

handsome and mesmerizing
drifting in an artificial world

they know each other
        companions friends perhaps
so alike in feather and foot
they could pass as brothers

I named one Wesley
indeed

a fitting name

and the other?
what is his name?

the wrong name may not describe him
very much a duck
he knows this

but I am unsure what to call him so on this pond he will
remain un-named
it is not my intention to offend

. . .

they glide lazy mirthful
I cannot tell them apart

they swim—lead follow
drift together

with no determined head
it is not always the oldest to lead
they care enough about the other not to get tangled with hierarchy

undirected and now apart the mallards swim

an argument?
respecting the other's need for space?

one
in true duckhood
preens his feathers
as does the other in spite of the distance

       quack

perhaps a friendly salutation?
or a broken plea?

Wesley returns to the other or the other returns to Wesley

that either would respond is all that matters now
with caring
feathered embrace uncommon for mallards
sadly too uncommon

Michael James

afloat the pond content to be silent
and be a duck

> together

> *quack quack!*

one of them leaves!

who was it that decided to go?

the other not moving now
ponds do not feel like home

conscious of his solitude
his pace quickens

no long effortless floating
instead active

determined and almost
frantic

coming to the reeds
he steps from the water

waddling and shimmies from his head to his tail
as only a duck can do

certainly attentive he is alone

quack

a lament or a prayer?

You are ready lad
go with blessings
I will be here

surely I cannot conclude that from a simple quack?

after all
Wesley and the other
the uncertain one
they are just

        ducks

mallards
two of them if I

remember correctly

Ha-Mayim min Ha-Shamyim

I

I hear the tumult of the raging seas
Your waves and surging tides sweep over me
In the storm with sheets of down-pouring

voda
        the wet fog and dew before dawn hiding
            roadsigns and turns

vand
        coolness embracing feet with delicate
            steps through the stream

vesi
        weight in pitcher as plants nourished with
            tender care

eau
        pools in the parking lot outside the bakery
            where baker sweeps

wasser
        clouds emptied above a dry land over tents
            and sandals

ruwa
        cold and served in a simple vessel by a
            bleeding woman

myim
        hot warm as tea or relaxation or washing

víz
        panting sticky fingers and sore knee
            humbled on mountain side

Un-Orthodox Boy

acqua

        sanctified in marble basin to purify with two fingers

vann

        golden bowl with brush and elderly black robed Seraphim

woda

        almost witness to drowning time slows down

água

        face inches above the surface with eyes closed

apa

        tears with salt rolling down

agua

        weeping and submersion under all around inviting forgiving

vatten

        witnessing beloved go under and return with smiles

su

Michael James

II

Flood rain pour store save wash clean drop

> deep current ocean sea river stream fjord dam

>> chaos amazing wonder renewal restoring

still raging power calm essential pure

> drink serve refill come life-giving holy

>> enduring satisfying cleansing compete covering flowing—Lord I need you!

panting longing streams and water and soul silent—O God

> thirst beauty desperate where when meeting come come flow

>> love dawn blessed-morn unfailing clear upon in all around—Lord!

sing and sleep rest stillness peace drink me deep—praying

> whispers breath tears and hurt and God gives life—gives water

Halcyon

Tenderly perched on long dead tree
Under such miserable drip of bleak rain
Our bird squatting, still with ruffled feathers
In perfect bird-like stance, alone in the wet
Precarious thunder, death cold wind
Heavens are rent with scarlet lightning
Clouds bleeding water as if wounded

Yet from our Kingfisher lord –
A slow blink of sharp dark eyes
A shimmy of his tail—a comical, delightful motion
Immovable, the bird has patience
Not yet the fourth watch of night
Sodden and soaked, vigilant he stays
Looking out into a world of chaos

Gently does he lift his head and look
As if searching for some signal from God
Then our bird still squatting with poise
Begins to sing to the tumultuous storm
Such melodic eerie song from he!
With ruffled feathers does he warble his spell

Briskly he jumps up on mystical wings
With unnatural speed, flies, soars, sails on the wind
The wet of Sir Kingfisher's feathers shine as lapis lazuli
More dancing than flight, he spins, spirals, and glides

Our Halcyon revealed! Enchanting a water-blue world
Then the Sun breaks this world of dark
Seas fall in slumber, winds return home no more to blow
Tranquil beauty once again, our bird-lord lands then shimmies his tail

Meddling with Water

Crossing a marble floor, boots echo in the vast chamber
Arched ceiling sleeping on pillars of blue alabaster
Decked and adorned with tapestry, cloth, paintings
High above, windowed dome lets golden light fill every corner

"I can make it rain"—he says with a grin
To demonstrate, a simple gesture of his right hand
Then plump grey clouds gather under the glass roof
Light rain falls, a delicate rainbow appears, for added effect

Well pleased, our magician stands below, only slightly damp
But a snap of the finger, and spoken word, inside weather stops
Another snap, his clothes dry, the room free of any water
His smile stretches from one end of the hall to the other

"You command the water as well do you not?"—so playfully asked
She agrees, and states—"I once filled your well upon your request"
An ornate bow,—"wonderful let's see what you can do now!"

She stands silent—"perhaps that would not be wise"

Continuing in playful poise, sir magician ask again, and again yet
She stands and looks, clearly fierce caution goes unnoticed
Wearing such warning like a shawl, her eyes wild with memory
Then, in a whisper of pain—"Very well . . . Monsieur"

She waves her right hand, then her left
With sharp precision, cuts through the air
Her eyes never leaving him, our sir magician
With voice quiet and hush in such a space, she chants her spell

Then, eyes wide and mouth gaping
Sir magician stares, entirely unprepared
Facing the wild roar of an ocean, the rage of a sea
Realizing only too late her warning, is then swept away

Ptarmigan

She the snow bird dwells
so far from

home

with glossy white feathers
and a carbon black beak
soon to grace

the winter sky
over icy plains and frozen stream
from east to west and

west some

more
to perch in the mountain crest
to sing her

longing lullaby

Deplore

tears of argent and sorrow linger
oh gentle rain!
falling in troves

each a heavy pearl
how precious thou art!

waters with a voice
singing loud its silent hymn
ever ringing like a clear dawn to the heart alone

oh dew on rosy fields
ebullient under thy brown eyes

fount behind and barred of memory
still the silver stain doth remain

Sitta canadensis

out in urban forest amidst trees of concrete and glass
there he finds memory

of nature
with cold november chill and heavy breath
sitting on bench of wood with bare trees
amidst
the stillness and quiet of city noise

he prays for he knows not what else to do
hurting heart racing,

where are you Lord?

looking up from hands cold wet with tears
bird hops upside on tree close yet far
captivated still he watches daring not to move
so small, so calm, so determined bird from God!

you come at hour of greatest need
then in silent wind, terrifying whispering
"are you not of more value than they?"

Offering

give me your fears
is what he
says
so
out from my pocket
i take a dirty
penny

toss it into the fountain

hits
the water
and sinks

i wish the water

was

not
so

clear

for i can still see the penny

Dance of the Elements

bright and blue a magic bird
old songs of water
sleeping within his feathers
he, the water charmer
perched in a large tree
alongside his company

golden and red another magic bird
the passion of fire
alive within her plumage
she, the fire bird
watches with intense dark eyes

an un-conventional pair
these two birds of

azure and crimson

so still they face one another
in some ancient dance

of fire and water

leaving the world to wonder
could the two ever really

mingle

Unwanted Splash

going along the path
stopping soon as
yonder is

                                      a lake

                     right in the middle of the road

curiously still

                  this is certainly a lake
                  right in the middle of the road

waiting at water–edge
for something

and patience honoured
now to cross

                stepping out onto the calling surface

                      walk on water!
            in bliss and love tread thereupon

                  out in the middle of a lake

                              yet

                           trip and

                            stumble
                    landing on knees and hands

turning around to the shore
looking to see what happened
what has undermined the waters?

                                seeing
                    terrible fear fills from head to foot
                                trembling

on the shore stands

The King!

            with eyes like fire and hair as lightning
            who has decided to throw rocks into the still
            waters

                        disturbing
                    marring the calm with

                    ripples and waves

            leaving a modern Peter to plea and scream
                    as he sinks into a sea
                    of doubts and uncertainty

Amour & Beauty

Wine

I have never had a glass
of wine something I have always wanted to try not
tasteful sips mind you some screed of a mouthful you
swish around then drown out with soda crackers

but a glass—filled

I have always wanted to try a glass of wine to learn and
understand what full bodied flavour actually means

a pure drink that only improves with age poured out in
beauty of liquid reds and plums

one day I shall have a glass of wine –

—then the bottle

yet for now the cork is to remain and the wax seal left
unbroken
I need to grow up first

Cavorting

Why would I take you here?
it's cold outside, and the

       trees are bare

I grin as the secret is guarded
until the moment is right
following the sounds in the branches

       then I stop

extend my hand and reveal the reason
I just love your expression;
some hybrid of
              intrigue,
      delight,
peace

certainly this *is* love –
me, the birds,
and you, my dear friend
all smiles as

God provides

Caramel Flavoured Dark Roast

Here a girl sits
across a brown-eyed boy

so eager to tell the mysterious inner-workings
of her heart
with fondness
misty forms fly in the coffee shop

-elusive creatures we call thoughts
or somesuch thing as a heartwarming

yet

business must drag forward and
with a simple switch
coffee grinder roars to life
in a rush of irritable noise
the soaring thoughts of a girl are
trampled and kicked
sealing her mouth shut
then sparking humour in the brown-eyed boy

causing him to smile at the expense

of her peevish expression
between them

both

their eyes

decreed the same tragedy that coffee

does not wait for love

Balance

I

days of sunshine
of cloudless sky
where dragonflies

in untold numbers take

wing
strange coloured ducks glide

effortless
cattails sway and poplar leaves dance
so alive is this world of

greens and blues

God is

King

II

days of sorrow
of cloudless sky
where on stone grave

never to take to wing

again
strange beautiful bird un-moving

still and at peace
creature sleep and poplar leaves dance
so dead in this body of

reds and browns

God is

King

Cloth

I have a scarf around my neck
fine weave of white, and black, and brown

for once I just look at my scarf
the grand pattern, the unique feel

how mysterious its creation
every thread shares a story

more complex that I had thought before

. . .

my scarf gives new meaning to things
fearfully and wonderfully made

Wednesday at 1 o'clock

tea is a must
in an April snowstorm

when mixing up pots
green ribbon or book clubs
with ice cream afterwards

at the granny–frequented table
in towns far away
exotic blends and new flavours

and of course

that wonderful noise
the *clink* of china

tn kitchens, campgrounds, shops
going and going again

always there is tea
poured out in love

Song of the Magpie

There stood the Magpie
just before my boots
as I stared motionless

>becoming wary of my presence
>he started to dance

well, realistically,
he hopped in random patterns

but to me it was a dance

as he bobbed and swayed
it occurred to me how fine his dress

in me formed a lament
for the bird who lives in a world

>where people like me throw rocks—
>cursing such birds as a nuisance

sensing my distain
he flourished his wings
then landed atop a letter box
only staying for two ticks
then flew out of sight

and I stood statuesque
chanting the chorus of a lament

oh annoying wonderful bird
do not let anyone call you
un-beautiful

Love So Great

oh such music . . . yes
head hung and eyes drawn like curtain—such music
statuesque
                      beautiful

sighs on crestfallen face melody of travails
as heart impedes and bleeds
alas dignified strains heard only by ears alone
utterly tormenting soon is this affliction

so thy dear music en pause –
frantic and broken, flees for intercession
pleas for something . . .
                               anything
and He gives . . .

                    (insert here)

                  . . . for His Love IS That Great

Academics

roses and snapdragons
bordered with dead poppies
some wilting thistles

here and there

the pungent
smell of a cigarette

somewhere

how often these roses
are missed

when soil turns
to concrete
and students meander
with heavy loads

of books

here at the institution
of learning

where minds are taught

not even to
notice
simple beauty

Faith & Ache

Driving the Dirt Road

Enter the bus
sit
fourth row from the front
slouch shoulders and
metal meet with disdain
exchange icy greetings,
and salutations
turn and look behind
chatter is somewhere
iPods are playing
search in the eyes of the
spread out group

would anyone know?
can they tell at just a
glance?
would the seeking one
even know what to find?
he says it's obvious
from the fourth row seat
he remembers

look over the faces see
waves of fatigue
exhaustion for some
listen to sounds of
earphones jealously
guarding their secrets
all things earthy betray
nothing
prince of air would have it
forgotten

yet that is not so!
for to those who care to
look—really look
treasure is found
unrelenting fire
now concealed by simple
time moving
some hours before

( )

[beauty embrace fire brokenness devotion healing

heart forgiveness conviction hands joy

life holy fullness in–description messages

pain light incomprehension meeting silence

song prayers love servants uncanny

verse surprising rhapsody tears word whispers surreal wonder wind]

( )

this should be nothing new
nothing they did not know before
after all it was only

Fellowship

Spin Straw into Gold

lie down child and
put your head to rest
frown in your sleep and
drink deeply the cold air

                        stare up into the darkness
                as you long to cry—but will not
                          hold my hand, child, and
                   let anguish sing you a lullaby

unsettled and unsure, rest easy tonight
you wonder to God why life is this way
to remember what is forgotten,
and to forget what is remembered

                            dream of going to the west,
                    though you traveled south instead

yes, child in the cold!
bring faces and
memory of disappointment or hurt

                            write in your book, and
                       collect your words in verse

oh child, sleep on in winter's chill
rest easy with grief,
child in the cold

                              sleep in the fortress where
                                   curses are blessings
                                   foolishly wise, so much
                                   you don't understand;

                such as when the Lord smiles at you.
                    shouldn't you smile back?

Tarnish

I

I remember then, a time . . . when I was new
how delicately you would look as quiet waves of delight
flowed in your eyes
ever lifting your hand to your face
colourful ribbons of caring unfold across your thoughts
so proud to tell my story to any who would listen
freely speaking with excited winds of praise blowing
from your heart
to be valued in such a way is so
perplexing

II

I remember then, at time . . . when I young
how devastated you were the first time I was careless
as silent tears of grief poured in your soul, still you did
not think lesser of me
incomprehensible
ashamed as again and again I would become careless
but you

did not give up
you still hoped and saw beauty beneath my many scars
unimaginable for

I was tarnished!

Oh how terribly deep and numerous were my scars!

yet you would make attempts to keep my shine bright

you spoke with bright fires of

renewal

burning in your voice

III

I remember then, a time … when I was old
you decided to intervene to remove my marks
and took painful action

cold nails
of forgiveness
pierced from
your hands

that you decide to refine
my mistakes is

unfathomable

IV

I remember then, a time . . . when I was made new
        how much brighter I shined and how different
        than before I looked
               you embraced me with deep wells of love
               flooding from your spirit

                        that my beauty was worth your
                        difficult choice is

                        precious

                        for now I am
                        purified

                I cling to your finger
                here I find solace

A Bird Then Gone

I

she wore a scarf
near the end of May

walking somewhere in the city
and there did she meet
such an elder of tenderness

she did not even have to consider the purchase
for the bird chirped and
warbled her sweet voice

a beautiful bird delicately laced
in her best of dresses –
elegant and with equanimity
a bird in a dress of

scarlet

II

he was wearing a bow tie
next week to come

taking hold of diaphanous cage
stroking the bird upon her head
with gingerly bent fingers

yet still was he compelled to
open the cage
and frown as the bird

flies not here

Captivated

The baker sweeps the floors
not at all wanting to work

so come then, outside

now he starts to mop
gritting his teeth in revolt

Come outside will you please?

unable to take anymore of this
the baker throws open the doors

and outside he is greeted with

rain

...Broken walls...
...Whispers...

...Voice...
...Love...

will you not come outside?

Arrow

The world is still
noiseless and whist
With judicious poise he follows in pursuit

He stops and looks . . .
                       . . . rewarded by keen eyes

    lying down on the cliffside—already wounded
    some hundred paces yonder—a far shot
    an arrow is drawn from his quiver

purple fletching
    black tipped
        he kisses the head

in such gesture of grace and beauty
draws back
he takes aim and . . . holds—ensuring his shot is perfect

. . .

longer than thought possible
he holds archer's stance
normally sinew and tendon would scream in revolt
he is strong—not even slightest betrayal of motion

a most insignificant flick of fingers is greeted with a heavy thud—

impossible
the release practically synonymous with sound
pierced deep—hurt and weak
no calling out or wail or even surprise

just the quick draw of hissed breath—and . . . tears
. . . from him who shot

        approaching the cliff
        hands reach down
lifting up his precious beauty—he closes his eyes

        remaining motionless
an eerie embrace of a dead thing and a man
        standing in a still world

        with blood on his hands

Adam Song

I should have been studying

but instead
I sat on my kitchen floor
      like a toddler

         scooping dirt into plastic pots
         and most gently transplanting hold
              sproutling worried and frightened

I sing deep lullabies to them slow

my hands dark with earth
imagining what it was like for

adam

learning to care for green things
as God holds
                  his tiny hands

Psalmofnosleep

Iwanttosleepbutonlytossandturnwithinme

    thedistantrumbleofacomingstormenoughreaso
reasonformyheartto

        remain alert a sickly wind blows beating dryempty trees

Icanbutstandandinwardlyfacenature'spoweraloneinthe night

    ohGodwillYouletmerest?

    myeyesstingfromthe

finesandtheairisdryandunpleasantlongingam

    Ijusttodreamwiththestars

Eucharist

In darken cathedrals, under
guard of coloured glass

the evening candles labour in
fields of gloom and coming night

close your eyes
drink of God's quiet wine

poured out in hymn and song
and in voice and in stones

water of life from altar's
storehouse is given

you weep as
you drink from the cup

drink deeply!
oh drink your fill!

under the watch of bronzed crucifix
you are embraced

stand and arise
stand and be silent!

be silent
be still!

Within the Attic

Falcons and robins abound in spring
pulling the tassels of longing

brown and dead grass is

      far spent a sight
springtime wounded and bitter
enough already!

disseminate the green
                        blue
            pink and
      yellow
to proliferate with the robins and falcons!

bleak and fragmented nature please
grow once more

somewhere

somewhere these tassels meet the corners
of tapestry
which is not covered in dust
and brown

and dead grass

Dream & Elusion

Lines Written in Response to a Children's Book

there it was
        and I saw it
                in a bookstore

a book
        yet this was
                a book among books

asking the world
        me, you
                to return to simpler
roots

Glámur - an Icelandic Song I Listened to

Some songs
are poetry

lacking lyrics
or voice
unfold in chimes
xylophones and sustained
chords somewhere a
violin
writes for me
a poem worth
reading again

leaving to ponder and chisel
how can I say what
music does
and the
poetry that comes
when you
listen?

My Memory in History

I. Playwright

I am trying to
       write a
              script narrating the life of
him

never personally known or even what he looked like
with only Anglo words and gestures he is to live again
breathe once more and shout through an ambitious
actor on a simple stage eons after he once did

II. Adoration

    how he must have cried as stone blocks dissolved
    into ruin
        yet he acquiesced to his Lord and the
        behest of grace

            salvation
            and hope

his words brought to a playwright an
idiosyncratic friendship with an embrace to traverse
quietly and in love
    the deep corridors

of so many years ago

Whatever-ness & Realisms

drowning in the sounds of keyboards, printers and office chatter
the calendar depicting a yellow-headed black bird perched on a cattail
and only twenty-three minutes until I am released
my neck aches
and my eyes are sad
interrupted by the ping of an email just received on muted computer speakers

I just don't know anything anymore

in the damp rain and 12°C outside air life slows in the sluggish
shuffle of an office
sad eyes just look around and try to think
casting a simple heavy look over to the plant I named

Malachi and gingerly a tilt of the head

    no more labels to remove
        my mundane task sits complete in filing bins
the mark of my efforts a shallow trophy of used green and white folders

just uneasy or depressed—it really does not a matter which

        now they are talking about winning Friday's lottery
I don't even bother to cock an eyebrow
it seems so pointless to consider, yet still it comes up in conversation

and then poking awake my sleepy computer
entering in the scripture password I have now memorized

        the verse does not ring in me today
though sad, that is the way it is as Isaiah utters encouragement to the people

        that God is here and He is guiding,
        strengthening, watering and so on

the latter, regrettable to consider or write with short pencil

they say that God is in the rain ... or at least in that movie she did

so praise God who is in the rain
yet my sad eyes blink
my mind thinks

whatever

Non-Wine Drinker

A clay goblet on a square table paired
with a small loaf of bread on silver plate
all atop a table cloth of black

one candle alight
a solitary   soul

waits his hands folded in hushed prayer eyes
closed to the

    world

uttering the amen he raises his right hand to
  trace the catholic cross

folding hands again he waits
quietly

a servant enters and walks near open a bottle of wine
letting smells of the drink fill the air as incense

spiced and sweetly vintage
nodding in approval for the selection
  fills the clay just above half and holds the bottle
  looks and waits

thanks are uttered courteously displayed as it should be
yet his hands are folded still

Michael James

as a surprised wine bearer bows in grace and flourish
> nodding to the glass and wordlessly implies to partake

he looks up then his hand goes to his coat to
check his pocket-watch returning a glance and
> shakes his head
>> not yet time to
>>> drink such

wine

Pens That Make Poems Better
for Sarah

and type
something and all
the while my glass
pen waits on
the shelf
shining with envy

Come, Green

As I write about a herd of deer

our thoughts

become one
from

across the valley

and through the windows
both the deer and myself

dream of springtime
and long for

green

The Question Still Stands

so oft my empty words fall

I do not know

can I truly plea ignorance?

or do I resist even entering the place
where a response can be given

merely rejecting the question

with a sheepish un-answer

At the Opera

Rain and rain

the slow quiet strains meld with the air

unopened roses shyly dress in wet lace

new saplings applaud with outstretched arms

the earth feels so

tired and worn out

so plays simple music with clouds

and green thanks

God

for the rain

My Prayer

I say it so often
wrapping my words for others
give them away
in all seriousness
or in jest
nevertheless,
true and honest

always with smiles
in the language of the heart

so it was a shock to see
that my brush is sticky and dry
my artist pallet is a mess with

paint

all running together
into sickly brownish hues

and I look at my hands
say nothing
once again fade into

black and white

I close my eyes
sing to whoever is
listening

please add the

colour

I need

Friend & Quirk

Childhood Fiddle-faddle

When I saw a rabbit
    who was, indeed,

white

        he was not wearing a waistcoat
        nor did he possess a watch

            in fact I cannot even be certain
            if he was not a she

yet still I smile as I walk briskly by

alone with a rabbit in the dark
who hops away at my passing

            with such eagerness to depart
            quite convincing that he was late

for something

or mayhaps i only smiled
because i wanted him

to be late

Un-Orthodox Boy

Whisper to the heart gently inward
voice come forward receive the joy of your

salvation I desire to share this with you
tonight put denomination aside and walk come

forward do not worry about the man of the
cloth I have told him to admit you your mark of jade is
enough for him your face is
recognizable at least to his eyes your

clumsy actions honour me and my

son Eat

Drink

Smile

we can have

fun together

dear

child

Publication

perhaps characters are perpetually frozen
until we turn the pages

    the cartoon cat is endlessly revealing his thoughts
    poets forever live in unread verse

        each book only exists in a reader's hands
        yet we continue to be animated, to live

            so then . . .
            one possible conclusion

                the author is reading his work

Follow Me

There was a cat this morning, so I gave it a pet; some tender scratches behind the ears
I made to leave, but the cat ran in front of me with each step I took

and in the afternoon, another cat!
different from the first, though same story: the cat running ahead of me as I made to leave

part of me wanted to follow after the cats; both of them
yet how could I? I am so clumsy; not quick on my feet
so instead I forgo such free and lazy adventures

to run across the road

Inquietude

looking out with dark brown eyes
        into not-complete darkness

        joined in fellowship under
                aegis of melody pure

Child of God sitting quietly
        beside Servant of God

        with gentle smile in
                veil of shadow are you greeted

unsure and almost uneasy,
        words crumble away into ash

longing that even such a sigh
        would be shared between us

        for frustration has been
                conquered by lament

song of sorrow who sings
        lullabies behind the walls

        but in breath dies upon the lips –
                I know not what to do nor say

Child of God, oh friend dear!
        help me find God's leading light of hope

      for it's a light dim—almost gone
          from dark eyes' vision

and though we sit
      in silence still and sweet

      wonder which of us
          such quietude will break

that words come back
      when suns do rise

      there with praise to our God,
          what then shall we say?

Perception

Silent grin and eyebrow raised
I see the ruby heart who sleeps

so quick the thought enters the mind
then escapes my lips in a

hiss of breath

I draw the knife from its resting sheath
these things must be done—delicately
reaching out with betraying gentle hand
tenderly touch with fingers

and . . . the knife sings its piercing song, swift!
murdered silent without waking

I stare at the scene before me
observing the bleeding over counter white

with beautiful poise I lay my knife
eyes dance as I rejoice upon the slain
feverishly begin to devour flesh of the fallen
delicious and sweet I savour the taste
thus is the timely end of

Pomegranate!

Within the Second Floor Vault

Who are you, I wonder

your name was just one of many
the first I took note of

it does not seem like you are real
yet you are a person in this world

you breath

and love –

cry

hope

prayers, tears

not bound by distance
one day I wish to meet you
I yearn see the

colour of your eyes

Deep Mistake

Just looked at my watch

I must know what
time of day it is
-
how long I have till
I must be somewhere that I am not now

yet with all this

distracted

and I put my watch back

remembering in a second
I still did not know the time

only to look once

more

Would God Fly a Kite?

Would God fly a kite today?
High in the sky and up in the heavens

Would the Lord run through a meadow?
Pulling a string and bounding with glee

Would the Great One dance in the sun
while paper soars?
When the wind sings its chorus and
chimes resound in the air

Will Abba our Father call to His children
with kite in His hands?
As He welcome us with bright smiles and
affectionate embrace

Would Jesus laugh and beam as he looks to
the sky?
Wanting to see just how high the kite will
go

Does Spirit echo happy refrains from
above the clouds and through the grass?
As trees and oceans bow in wonder of His
passing by

Does I AM simply want to play and
delight ... with us?

Well I flew a kite with Daddy today . . .
I was the kite and Jesus the string
Spirit the wind and Abba the Anchor . . .

Holding on tight and who never lets go

More Than a Poem

Such odd quirks are
there beneath
– the hidden nuances of poetry
how often do we watch the
birth of
       a
               poem?

embroidered within a select choice of words are
fingerprints only
revealed if the pen speaks of them
in the vast collection of a wordy landscape lies the sleeping undisclosed choreography and we
we are given but a page a thought a(n)

(un)completed text by authors

         who more often
    than
not

do not disclose such poetics—these things being the text of poetry

indeed the embossing of the process—the journey
moves us to wonder—maybe even smile—at the quirky
mannerisms

the strikingly unconventional traits

and the poetry
        that
                it
                          creates

CPSIA information can be obtained at www.ICGtesting.com
Printed in the USA
LVOW092325290312

275333LV00001B/50/P